SPOTLIGHT ON CIVIC ACTION

SOCIAL ACTIVISM

WORKING TOGETHER TO CREATE CHANGE IN OUR SOCIETY

BEATRICE MORTMAIN

PowerKiDS press™

NEW YORK

Published in 2018 by The Rosen Publishing Group, Inc.
29 East 21st Street, New York, NY 10010

Editor: Theresa Morlock
Book Design: Michael Flynn
Interior Layout: Tanya Dellaccio

Photo Credits: Cover Simon Ritzmann/Photodisc/Getty Images; pp. 4, 6, 7, 9 Bettmann/Getty Images; p. 5 Mario Tama/Getty Images News/Getty Images; p. 10 Central Press/Hulton Archive/Getty Images; p. 11 Robert W. Kelley/The LIFE Picture Collection/Getty Images; p. 12 JNix/Shutterstock.com; p. 13 AFP/Getty Images; p. 15 Fotosearch/Archive Photos/Getty Images; p. 16 New York Post Archives/The New York Post/Getty Images; p. 17 SAUL LOEB/AFP/Getty Images; p. 19 Steve Exum/FilmMagic/Getty Images; p. 21 Hurst Photo/Shutterstock.com; p. 22 Blend Images/Shutterstock.com; p. 23 NurPhoto/Getty Images; p. 25 2p2play/Shutterstock.com; p. 27 Adam Davy - PA Images/Getty Images; p.29 Rick Diamond/Getty Images Entertainment/Getty Images.

Cataloging-in-Publication Data

Names: Mortmain, Beatrice.
Title: Social activism: working together to create change in our society / Beatrice Mortmain.
Description: New York : PowerKids Press, 2018. | Series: Spotlight on civic action | Includes index.
Identifiers: ISBN 9781538327944 (pbk.) | ISBN 9781508163985 (library bound) | ISBN 9781538328064 (6 pack)
Subjects: LCSH: Youth--Political activity--Juvenile literature. | Social action--Juvenile literature.
Classification: LCC HQ799.2.P6 M67 2018 | DDC 320.40835--dc23

Manufactured in China

CPSIA Compliance Information: Batch #BW18PK For further information contact Rosen Publishing, New York, New York at 1-800-237-9932.

CONTENTS

CHAPTER ONE

A HISTORY OF CHANGE

Social **activism** has played an important role in the development of our society and system of government over time. Social activists identify injustices in society and the government and work to fix them. There have been several key social movements in American history. In this book you'll learn about three major movements that brought about reform to the way the U.S. government and society operate—the Progressive

WOMEN'S SUFFRAGE MARCH, 1915

WOMEN'S MARCH ON WASHINGTON, 2017

Many of the methods used by social activists throughout history are still used today. Marches and demonstrations are used to raise awareness about a number of issues.

movement, the civil rights movement, and the disability rights movement.

There are many social movements at work today. By considering historical examples of such movements, the means they used to effect change, and how their successes have improved America, we can learn how to use social activism to address problems in our modern society.

CHAPTER TWO

THE PROGRESSIVE MOVEMENT

One of the major social movements in the United States occurred between 1890 and 1920. This period came to be called the Progressive Era.

During the 19th century, the United States experienced huge industrial growth, which led to many social and political problems. Factory workers were often forced to work in unsafe and unhealthy conditions.

This photo shows steel workers on strike in Chicago, Illinois, in 1919. Workers went on strike to protest the poor working conditions and low wages.

Eugene Debs was one of the champions of the Progressive movement. Debs supported unionism, which is the practice of uniting workers to obtain better working conditions through collective action.

Corporate bosses used any means necessary to make money without concerning themselves with public welfare. Corrupt, or dishonest, political leaders created a great economic divide between the classes.

The Progressive movement was a response to problems brought about by the industrial boom. During this time, social activists focused on addressing issues such as workers' rights, corporate greed, and political corruption. Their efforts brought about social and political reforms that continue to benefit American citizens today.

CHAPTER THREE

THE MUCKRAKERS

Muckraking was one of the most effective tools used by progressive reformers. Muckrakers were **journalists** and other writers who investigated and exposed corruption and wrongdoing in business and government by providing detailed accounts to the public. Muckraker journalism uncovered the truth about problems in society and gained support for reforms. For example, Upton Sinclair's novel *The Jungle*, published in 1906, revealed information about the meat-packing industry and helped lead to the passage of the federal Pure Food and Drug Act of 1906 and the Meat Inspection Act of 1907.

For the social activists of the Progressive movement, muckraking proved to be an effective means of creating social reform. Today, investigative journalists use the same methods to uncover problems and bring about reforms.

Ida Tarbell was a muckraker who wrote about John D. Rockefeller's Standard Oil Trust in 1904. Tarbell's work helped lead to regulations on industries and break up the Standard Oil Trust.

CHAPTER FOUR

THE CIVIL RIGHTS MOVEMENT

The civil rights movement of the 1950s and 1960s is a major example of social activism in American history. After the Civil War (1861–1865), southern states enacted laws to **segregate** the races and **oppress** African Americans. The civil rights movement was a collective effort to resist these unjust practices and

Some civil rights activists were inspired by Mohandas Gandhi's teachings about nonviolent resistance. Gandhi was a social activist who successfully led the Indian independence movement, which ended in 1947.

This picture was taken in August 1963 when civil rights activists marched in Washington, D.C. Both white and black people were involved in the civil rights movement.

others. Activists came together to bring about reforms that would work against the system of **discrimination** and establish legal equality for African Americans.

Much civil rights activism took place at the grassroots level. That means that ordinary people made up a large part of the movement. Organizations such as the Southern Christian Leadership Conference led by Martin Luther King Jr. created a framework for grassroots activism. Grassroots activism involved participation in direct action such as nonviolent protests and civil disobedience.

CHAPTER FIVE

DIRECT ACTION

Direct action was a key part of civil rights activism. Civil rights activists resisted the unjust system by refusing to cooperate with it. Rosa Parks sparked the Montgomery bus boycott when she refused to give up her seat to a white man on a segregated bus in 1955. The bus **boycott** lasted for 381 days and resulted in the desegregation of Montgomery city buses.

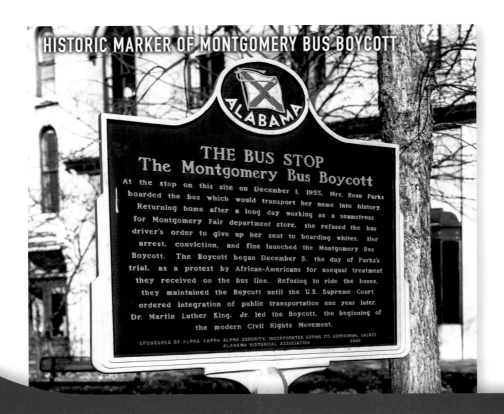

HISTORIC MARKER OF MONTGOMERY BUS BOYCOTT

This photo shows Martin Luther King Jr. and civil rights supporters at the March on Washington in Washington, D.C., in 1963.

By staging massive demonstrations, activists were able to draw attention to problems in the community and propose solutions. In 1963, over 200,000 activists marched through the nation's capital to the Lincoln Memorial during the March on Washington. It was during this march that Martin Luther King Jr. made his famous "I Have a Dream" speech. The march laid the foundation for the Civil Rights Act of 1964.

CHAPTER SIX

THE DISABILITY RIGHTS MOVEMENT

Today, one in five Americans has a disability. For a long time people with disabilities have been misunderstood and discriminated against. Disabilities can take many different forms and affect people of all backgrounds. The goal of the disability rights movement is to raise awareness about issues people with disabilities face. The movement also works to **integrate** people with more severe disabilities, who have often been segregated from society, with the public.

The disability rights movement began to take shape during the 1960s. One of its main goals was to change society's understanding of disability. People with disabilities don't wish to be treated with pity. The disability rights movement seeks to create conditions in which people with disabilities can live independent, fulfilling lives and actively participate in society.

President George H. W. Bush signed the Americans with Disabilities Act into law in 1990. The act protects the civil rights of people with disabilities.

CHAPTER SEVEN

CHALLENGING PERCEPTIONS

For many years, barriers prevented people with disabilities from gaining equal access to facilities and programs. For example, some buildings only had stairs, which made it difficult or impossible for people in wheelchairs to enter. Blind or deaf people were excluded from certain programs.

Alba and Anastasia Somoza are twin sisters who both use wheelchairs. In 1994, their parents began a court case to fight for better school services for students with disabilities.

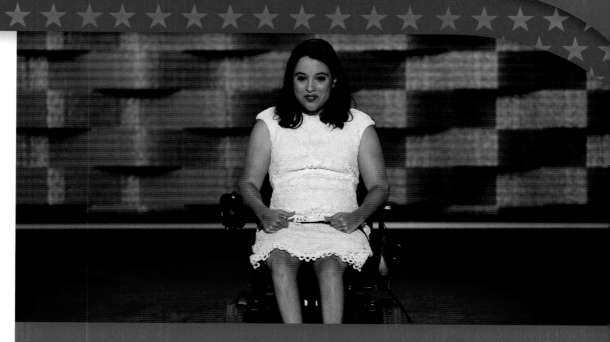

Anastasia Somoza has continued to fight for the rights of disabled people throughout her life. In 2016, she spoke at the Democratic National Convention in Philadelphia, Pennsylvania.

Ed Roberts was a social activist who worked to show people that disability issues are civil rights issues. He argued that people with disabilities have the right to live independently and make decisions about their own lives. Roberts's work helped bring about legal reforms to promote independence for people with disabilities.

Like the civil rights activists, activists for disability rights held demonstrations that brought their issues to the public eye. They blocked buses that weren't accessible, staged **sit-ins** in government buildings, and participated in marches.

CHAPTER EIGHT

MODERN SOCIAL ACTIVIST MOVEMENTS

In some ways, the social movements that we've examined here are ongoing. The Black Lives Matter movement could be seen as an extension of the civil rights movement. This movement addresses unfair treatment of African Americans, such as **racial profiling**. The LGBT movement also expands on issues of equal rights for all. This movement focuses on social and legal equality for lesbian, gay, bisexual, and **transgender** people.

Although the concerns of social movements vary greatly, the unifying goal of many is to improve existing systems of government and build a society in which all people are treated with respect. Are you aware of any social causes that affect you or someone you know? You can lend your support to a cause even if you aren't directly affected by it.

Love is Love
Women's Rights are Human Rights
Climate Change is Real
Black Lives Matter
Immigrants Make America Great

This woman's sign shows the modern social activist issues she supports.

CHAPTER NINE

STEPS OF SOCIAL ACTIVISM

Social activism can be broken down into several steps. The first step is to identify the problem. We'll use the problem of pollution as an example. Next, you must consider what causes the problem. Throwing away too much trash is one of the main causes of pollution. The next step is to think about what changes citizens could make to fix this problem. We can reduce the negative effects of this type of pollution by recycling and using reusable items.

A major step in any social activist campaign is raising awareness. The more people know about a problem, the better they're able to help solve it. Social activists raise awareness about pollution by spreading information about its causes and negative effects. Raising awareness about a problem also helps you gather support.

You can help reduce the negative effects of pollution by being mindful of how much trash you create. When you work to fix a problem in society, you are practicing activism.

The next step is to figure out what methods will be most effective in bringing about the change you wish to see. Social activists working to solve the issue of pollution try to bring about legal reforms by **lobbying**, signing **petitions**, and voting for representatives who support their cause. They may also hold marches and demonstrations to express their concerns to the government and the public.

The choices you make every day can be a form of social activism. You may decide to buy reusable shopping bags to reduce the amount of plastic bags that get thrown away.

     Although social activism is a collective effort to bring about change, one of the biggest ways to contribute to a cause is by changing your own behavior to reflect your beliefs. If you want to fix the problem of pollution, you can make decisions about how you live your own life and reduce the amount of pollution you put into the world.

CHAPTER TEN

WAYS YOU CAN HELP

You can make a difference in your community, country, and the world no matter how old or young you are. There's work for everyone in a social movement!

Is there an issue that you feel strongly about? You might be passionate about protecting the environment. You could be interested in protecting animals and their rights. Maybe you or someone you know is experiencing discrimination. You have the power to make the changes you wish to see in society.

Think about how your choices can help fix a problem that you see. Inform people around you about the problem and how you think it could be fixed. Write to your representatives in the local, state, and federal governments. Organize or participate in a march. Share your knowledge about the cause.

If there's a cause you feel strongly about, research it. Watch informative films, read books and articles, and learn as much as you can so that you can make an informed decision about how to fix it.

CHAPTER ELEVEN

ACTIVISM ONLINE

The Internet is a great resource for spreading awareness and gathering support. The Internet makes it possible for people throughout an entire country or the world to participate in a social activist movement. Activists can become involved by donating money to a cause, speaking out on social media, or signing online petitions. You can also help organize boycotts, marches, and other demonstrations by sharing information about them online.

Social media is a perfect place to spread information about social causes. You can encourage your friends and followers to learn more about an issue by creating a website or short video and providing links to websites or articles with additional information on the subject. Using social media in the right way can turn a small movement into an internationally supported cause.

Many modern movements use a catchy phrase and hashtag to popularize their cause. The phrase #WeStandTogether, pictured here, is part of a campaign in the United Kingdom to celebrate everyone's differences.

CHAPTER TWELVE

CAREERS IN SOCIAL ACTIVISM

There are more ways to become involved in social activism than volunteering or participating online. Certain careers allow citizens work to influence society and government policies. If you become a lawyer, you may be able to take cases that involve civil rights. By becoming a social worker or a doctor, you could work directly with people in need of support or **advocate** for their needs.

A career in social activism could mean working directly with individuals or discovering the causes of problems in society and finding ways to solve them. For example, one social activist could help homeless people find places to live. Another social activist could research the problems in society that make it difficult for people to find jobs and afford homes.

Many social activists work for social justice, which is the belief that all people deserve respect and equality. John Lewis, pictured here, was a civil rights leader in the 1960s and is now a U.S. congressman.

CHAPTER THIRTEEN

BE THE CHANGE

The actions of a single person can bring about changes that help thousands. Every social movement in history has begun with the work of just a few people. Although working toward social change can feel overwhelming, it's important to remember that the choices you make every day can make a difference. What are some changes you could make to help create a better society?

First, think about the way your behavior affects other people. You can create a more just and fair society by treating everyone around you with respect and valuing your differences. You can become a more **compassionate** person by talking to people who are different from you and learning about their experiences. The greatest tools of social activism are communication, determination, and a vision for a better future.

GLOSSARY

activism (AK-tih-vih-zum) Acting strongly in support of or against an issue.

advocate (ADD-voh-kayt) To support or argue for a cause or policy.

boycott (BOY-kaht) A refusal to buy, use, or participate in something as a form of protest.

compassionate (kuhm-PAA-shuh-nuht) Showing or feeling kindness or understanding.

discrimination (dis-krih-muh-NAY-shun) Different—usually unfair—treatment based on factors such as a person's race, age, religion, or gender.

integrate (IN-tuh-grayt) To make a person or group part of a larger group.

journalist (JUHR-nuh-list) A person who collects, writes, or edits news for newspapers, magazines, television, or radio.

lobby (LAH-bee) To attempt to influence government officials to make certain decisions.

oppress (uh-PRESS) To treat cruelly or unfairly.

petition (puh-TIH-shun) A formal written request to a leader or government, usually signed by many citizens, regarding a particular cause.

racial profiling (RAY-shul PRO-fy-ling) The use of race as grounds for suspecting someone of having committed a crime.

segregate (SEH-grih-gayt) To set one group apart from others because of race, religion, class, or gender.

sit-in (SIT–in) A protest in which people sit or stay in a place and refuse to leave.

transgender (tranz-JEN-duhr) A person whose gender identity is different from the anatomy they were born with.

INDEX

PRIMARY SOURCE LIST

Page 7
Eugene V. Debs making a speech. Photograph. By International News Photos, 1912. Now kept at International News Photos, 235 East 45th Street, New York, New York.

Page 9
Ida M. Tarbell. Photograph. By Harris & Ewing. Between 1905 and 1945. Now kept at the Library of Congress Prints and Photographs Division Washington, D.C.

Page 16
Anastasia, Alba, and Gerardo Somoza at the Board of Education in Brooklyn, NY. Photograph. By Spencer A. Burnett, March 25, 1994. Now kept at the New York Post Archives.

WEBSITES

Due to the changing nature of Internet links, PowerKids Press has developed an online list of websites related to the subject of this book. This site is updated regularly. Please use this link to access the list: www.powerkidslinks.com/sociv/activism